gospel
OF A
whole sun

Andrews McMeel Publishing
a division of Andrews McMeel Universal
1130 Walnut Street, Kansas City, Missouri 64106

www.andrewsmcmeel.com

24 25 26 27 28 TEN 10 9 8 7 6 5 4 3 2 1

ISBN: 978-1-5248-8980-7

Library of Congress Control Number: 2023947895

ATTENTION: SCHOOLS AND BUSINESSES
Andrews McMeel books are available at quantity
discounts with bulk purchase for educational,
business, or sales promotional use. For information,
please e-mail the Andrews McMeel Publishing
Special Sales Department: sales@amuniversal.com.

gospel OF A whole sun

KATERINA JENG

Andrews McMeel
PUBLISHING®

Cover art illustrated by Gentle Oriental, aka
Gabrielle Widjaja, a queer, Asian, Brooklyn-
based creative who explores abstract feelings
about life & identity through mediums such as
graphic design, illustration, and tattoo.

For every person
finding their way

Table of Contents

Incantation	1
SHE SAID YES!	2
Hell Is a Funhouse Mirror	3
Aspirations I	4
Coming of Age	6
Compose Message	8
Home Has Never Been a Place	9
Mandatory Order	12
Soft Power	14
Happy Anniversary	15
I Am an Ocean Tide	17
What Happens When I Stop Asking Them?	18
Tomorrow I Am Golden	20
I Need to Stop Baking Cakes for Insecure Men	21
Freedom Dreaming	23
Ritual	25
Mourning After	28
Letter from Anonymous	32
In Bloom	34
Freedom	36
Aspirations II	38
2 a.m. Poem	39
I Say Goodbye	40
Year of the Tower (XVI)	42
For the Aunties	45
When It Floods	49
Love Is a Revolution	50
Buffet of Boys	52
I Love the Trees in Brooklyn	54

Dreamstate   58
How the Clouds Waited   59
I Love You Beyond   63
She Was (We Are) Christina Yuna Lee   65
Aspirations III   70
My Beating Red   71
How to Forgive a Soul   72
Prayer   74
Tree Glitter   75
Dark Fantasies   77
Meet You There?   79
M2 to Københavns Lufthavn   81
This, Too, Will Become a Memory   82
I Actually Miss America?   84
When Friendship Becomes Art   87
How to Escape the Matrix   89
Morning Coffee Is a Portal   92
Really Really Really Really Really Sad Poem   95
Recipe for Healing   97
Asian American: An Etymology   102
Immigrant Gluttony   105
And Still, Bliss   108
Perennial   111
Be My Guest   112
I Am the Whole Sun   115
The Best Human on Earth   116
On Our Way   120
Notes   123
Acknowledgments   129

let the portal be open
let the channel be clear
may what is meant to be said through me appear

let the portal be open
let the channel be clear
may what is meant to be said through me appear

let the portal be open
let the channel be clear
may what is meant to be said through me appear

let the portal be open
let the channel be clear
may what is meant to be said through me appear

let the portal be open
let the channel be clear
may what is meant to be said through me appear

let the portal be open
let the channel be clear
may what is meant to be said through me appear

let the portal be open
let the channel be clear
may what is meant to be said through me appear

let the portal be open
let the channel be clear
may what is meant to be said through me appear

Incantation

These words	These words
are windows to within—	a compass,
gateways,	for those to come
They hold spells	to dream while awake
portal to home and heaven	carry to realms in slumber
A harvest	A birthright in
coming	home.

SHE SAID YES!

This gargantuan diamond is a distraction from the fact that america doesn't teach you to say anything other than *yes!* and why aren't I crying with my foot popped and isn't this the moment I've been waiting for my entire girlhood and I'm not sure how to measure years of entanglement in minutes but I guess "the next step" is for him to legally claim me and I'm not sure where my voice is but at least I can feel the faintest heartbeat . . .

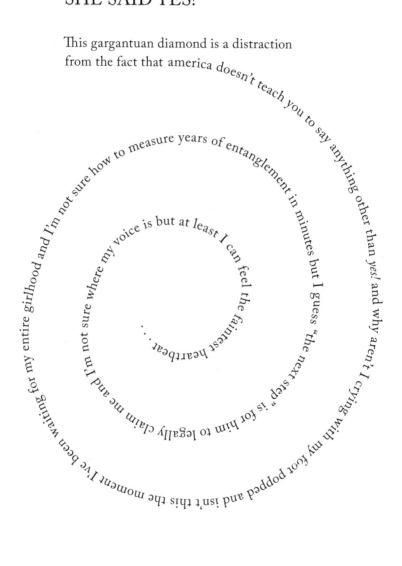

Hell Is a Funhouse Mirror

His rage
is stunning
topsy-turvy madness
from a man I do not know

It is blood running down shins
a hole in the staircase wall
our memories torn, belongings piled
to form a mountain of shame

It is poison seething
between teeth
verbal warfare on repeat
and the rifle is automatic
so when I've gone
limp and no longer
understand who I am
it still does not stop

I want to stay
I am shaking

I want to stay
but he shoves me out the door

Aspirations I

She is made of jade:

a precious gem with edges that do not cut

and a color so remarkably translucent

that even her flaws are brilliant

Is it wrong to be selfish
in a life that is yours?

Coming of Age

When you become a woman,

they tie your wrists with rope.

It's easy to smile sweetly, spin silk with your words,

but what they fear most is the sorcery your hands can conjure

You can shake the heavens with your will,

rumble the earth with sass,

breathe color into wasteland, life into slumber

And once you are here, sis, it is a glorious view.

Let me share secrets:

it's best to break free with swift precision—

sharp shears will suffice,

though even with immaculate escape

they will still call you angry

Your pain is as real as the dirt beneath your nails.

I know this to be true

because your pain is mine, too

The rope, however,

is of a different thread:

it is only as real as the light of the moon.

Compose Message

hey, happy day! / just / checking in / sorry to

bother / hope i'm not! / no rush at all / yes /

following up / noticing / curious as to / wondering

when you might / if you've had the chance / are you comfortable

in your chair? did you spend seconds considering

my careful composition? is my note

wow! so amazing!! or is it melting my agency

into a translucent ceiling? it's interesting how solid

a surface so quick to shatter appears—

invisible boundary that traps us below

typing and deleting, typing and deleting

until language is left lifeless,

programmed within

without our will.

Home Has Never Been a Place
after "Portable Cities" by Sally Wen Mao

Leaf through my pages, dwell in my nests

but be forewarned—oasis was never found

on a map. Outsider in origin

finds refuge in invisible cities

portable family, comfort constructed

safety in the in-between . . .

won't you come with?

*

Long Island held divorce in its sprawling homes

empty wings reluctant basins of grief

school a kennel club of ivory that bleached

the beauty of color—I didn't understand back then

why Sunmi, whose yellow rivaled mine

stopped seeing me. Sunmi, who taught me

the game of *gonggi*, rainbow plastic in the air

Sunmi, whose house I rode to at dusk

as the trees turned black and white

Sunmi, whose mother cackled

as I opened the small fridge for exiled kimchi
and exhaled, *mmm, that smells good.*

*

For four summers I lived in a snow globe
though Ithaca didn't need shaking to show
a torrent of tests, informational deluge
blurred lines, gulps of booze
where sisterhood said *cut that bitch*
strawberries begged to be picked
a city of falls frozen with memory
I have grown too worthy to relive

*

I learned from Ma in New York
metropolis of extremes—
salt-soaked skin or cheek-numbing wind—
toward the Bronx or Queens
they're either family or stranger, but nevertheless
the concrete always shimmered when she simmered
rice water, ginger, Mama Sita's tamarind

she said boil first what takes longest to soften—

pork spareribs, cause a little fat is good

add tomato, white radish, onion, in chunks

sitao, finger-length, fleshy fish head last

simmer with patience, stir and stir

favor flavor over measuredness

staples over opulence, she said you'll know

it's ready when everything is tender—

all you need to do is taste.

Mandatory Order

Last night I woke while the moon still hung
thoughts tearing apart my mind like headlines to humanity

But my body lay still with an unmistakable message:
it told me to call my family

Civilization is relearning to care—
to know thy neighbor, give to strangers

Love the ones who brought us to life
like these could be the last moments of theirs

Surge of questions, ancient and tall
despite the wreckage, seismic shifts reveal all

When the world is drowning
and we can't breathe

Know that to escape a tsunami
requires rising to safety.

Never mind the to-do list . . .

what is, deeply
your to-do?

Soft Power

They say I'm not strong because they can't fathom
a woman sweet as honey that blooms in boiling water
a voice so melodic that truth hits harder in her timbre
and a softness that makes the toughest armor crumble

I move slowly to gather strength
for magic needs divine timing
I am silent, for intuition speaks
more truth than one thousand words
I choose rest to resist cycles that oppress
for justice is a place to lay your head

Softness is the prize for resilience
patron of evolution
a kind way to get what you want
potent spell for taking what you need

So stay sweet, sis
the space is yours
ants in a colony work instinctually for their queen
who reigns with servitude

Happy Anniversary

In one year I cracked open
nested with grief
befriended my devils
awoke to angels
wove with words
found freedom in clippers
fiction in labels
possibility in both
In one year I learned truth
crowned my body
relieved my "musts"
learned to rest
stopped the running
found beauty in darkness
divinity in routine
the sun within
In one year I grew futures
chipped at noise
kindled my voice
surfed the swells
tuned the input
tilled the soil
to sow the seeds, once more

"Failure is the mother of success."
—fortune cookie wisdom

I Am an Ocean Tide

I want

to worship

your gravity to pull me into orbit

your tongue to leave me speechless

for I am an ocean tide

serene in delivery

but thundering

and utterly controlled by you

What Happens When I Stop Asking Them?

Remember when we escaped
the dank Manhattan drizzle
seeking answers from aunties
in cramped Chinatown refuge?

How our auras were identical—
indigo and magenta in rosy swirl
you're in love, yet
my essence was hazy with wear?

What color am I
uninterrupted, oozing like
blueberries baked hot
in a deep dish of my own ripeness?

A verdant green, rooted
in ever-present knowing?
A yolky orange, fertile
with unborn creation?

What alchemy occurs
when I give oxygen to anger?
Who am I in the absence
of men?

Women don't exist to jump
from the hands of man to man.

—note to self, post-therapy

Tomorrow I Am Golden

Tomorrow I don earrings of the *donya Ate Heather* sculpted

last time I needed to be reborn

illustrious matriarch loops my lobes, bends of women adorn

my fingers as my body drips heavy with protection

Tomorrow I summon my bloodline,

the mothers who shape-shifted to survive

let them rejoice at witnessing the freedom

that was rationed for them like wartime gasoline

Tomorrow I remember I am no man's queen

for I am the kingdom

rich in magnificence, innately worthy

reigning over what is already mine

I Need to Stop Baking Cakes for Insecure Men

it was like we decided to bake a cake! and you were too busy with so-called fancy people on so-called fancy calls and the black hole of your own ego so I baked the entire! cake! myself! and this was a *great-british-bakeoff*-level cake! there were layers of macerated blackberries and my deepest-hued plums and raspberry-red frosting because I didn't know how to give any less! than my garden's most precious fruit! and as I labored, you droned on & on about how you, translucent man, had the right to wear a shirt that said "fuck the system" with two vagina-owners fingering each other! argued over how it made me, actual vagina-owner, want to crawl out of my skin! argued over your "daddy" hat, which is only subversive when someone other than a white man wears it! argued over all the unarguable things men like you love to debate with women like me—women who cater, women who give, women whose color is seen as capital—so thank god you rage-quit! thank paul & mary you never made it to the finale because I just might've kept baking you cakes forever!

see the flags.

Freedom Dreaming

I want to bathe in enoughness

    rinse expectation

        from my hair

    soak safety into pores

        as womb of warmth

           returns me to worth

I want to   catnap

           in sunbeams

relax

in the protest of rest

    let my skin agree with sun

        whose setting

          is my only clock

I want each meal to be a sacrament

each sunrise a baptism

each touch a blessing

each exchange an act of care

I want to see love
sovereign

lush and wild—

growing even

in the places we forget

Ritual

Before noon

I worship breath

whirl the night's weight

until I am born again

Sharp sun creates cathedral—

my home, a church

and I am charmed

by Coltrane & Sanders,

chant of tanpura & harp

Bewitched,

I grip the hips

of an hourglass

seduced by steam,

submissive to first sips

of that holy, caramel water

A sometimes sacrament

of eggs & toast

but always confession—

I part scripture,

put pen to page

and the spirit

takes my body

unraveling, until

the words become undone.

The universe speaks to those who listen.

Mourning After

Normally I get a gentle greeting

sticky sap & spotting coaxing me to rest

but the morning after

the Atlanta gunman murdered my sisters,

my cycle came early

bright, viscous blood painted the toilet bowl

with a furious vengeance, thick grief

of ancestral ache

layered onto my womb

over lifetimes

The morning after,

the media seized my friends—

the same institution that shields stories of whiteness

invaded our sacred space

to hurry mourning

how dare they

ask us to process our pain for them?

how dare they

demand help with work they should have

been doing over centuries?

The morning after,

my ex texted me—

the one I closed the door on

because Asian women

were telling me things he was saying

to Asian women

I was furious

at the invitation to find comfort in him

I was furious

at the rich man who came twice

and left me empty

who smiled as he told me he took

an Asian woman's virginity once

I feel my insides slide out of me

and all I can do is listen

to my womb, terrorized

with rage, bleeding out

the morning after they did

without warning, knowing

the sameness

of our blood

your gut feeling = your ancestors speaking

Letter from Anonymous

He mailed me a letter typed in Calibri
titled "10 Things We Hate About You,"
and as I read its violent words,
checked the locks,
and called my mother,
I thanked God I got out
and I saw him,
a little boy, sitting on the floor
clipping   R

               A

                      N

                               S

                                     O

                                               M

from a magazine

you
are your most
important source of:

validation
wisdom
healing
care
romance
love

In Bloom

There is a spring becoming inside me
and I want to fall in love
with every blossom, some budding
into words I hope
hang in heaven, others sprouting
green abundance, each growing
in its own time, fragments
that compose
a magnificent garden
I am dizzy
for a man who says *thank you*
when I kiss his neck
fevered with texts twirling and
pages scrawled with half-baked—
bumble bees sprinkling
into divine sticky centers
of each flower
to flower
when I buried my lists
out bloomed measures,
new ways to deem a day
worthy
what am I watering?
how to tend
to a whole garden flourishing?
and amidst the frenzy

knowing
that I want to ripen
with only those who love my roots
for my flowers
wither each winter
and emerge with new hues
shapes unimaginable until they become
each spring, time and time again

Freedom

A reckoning
        with the four walls that enclose you
                    rot festering in misshapen ceiling
                    and a crumbling brick foundation
        that heaves and sobs more violently each passing year

A realization:
            architects of a dilapidated house
            will never wield the tools you require

You are blessed with wings and range—
why fix windows and doors when
you have infinite
blue sky?

"We are the leaders we've been looking for."

—Grace Lee Boggs

Aspirations II

She is made of jade:

a gem whose brilliance is in knowing

how she cuts, the precision

in her flaws, that the jewels will find her

remarkable—just as she is.

2 a.m. Poem

Do all poets fall in love
as easily as I do?
They must.

For poets are tasked with honesty
palms open, we let life's fruit
land in gentle grasp

I want your ripest peach
the one with the bruises
the one that has been lounging in sun

I bite into lush flesh
let nectar drip down fingertips
delight in tartness on my tongue

And just as I picked you,
I lay you down
witness to your pleasure and your grief
your yearning to be free
and because of it, I fall.

I Say Goodbye

and I morph
another adornment lacing lobes
small revolution found
in clipping fifteen inches
snake outgrowing skin
inked on mine to symbolize
death and birth
death and birth, eternal
reminder that finding joy means finding ease
amid our constant state of groundlessness.

solitude ≠ loneliness

Year of the Tower (XVI)

Today I praise sticky

new york subway lust,

lightning dancing

on city skyline, iconic

manhattan glamour on top of

The Standard, me

on top, in heat of July, tramping

through fort greene in my silk

cream center-slit skirt,

exorcism of thirst—added oil

to my stepford life

until it combusted and I,

aflame, free-falling

out of The Tower

as it burned down

around me. When men

asked why I destroyed

the Pinterest-perfect wedding,

I couldn't find language,

because how can one speak

when choking on smoke?

But time is a mother

and as I gathered my pieces,

nestled even the shards,

I saw the fire as initiation,

igniting my reincarnation.

It doesn't have to be perfect.
It just has to be honest.

For the Aunties

I love reading menus with B—anticipatory

love language, like when Enriqueta, Cuban *abuela*

dripping in jewels and big white hair,

saw us arrive at her sandwich shop, cut through

the clamor with her finger pointed toward us, ordered,

SIT, and we felt at home in Miami,

being barked at by an elder with love

Café con leche evaporada, *jugo de guayaba*

tostada y lechon especial for breakfast,

and as the plates rolled out we began

our descent into gluttony;

neither of us drink much so instead

we cheers our *empanadas d'espinacas*,

pile food onto the other's plate, no words

just noises and one more bowl of rice

and they move us to a larger table because

we take space and six *croquetas* to-go

I could listen to A talk about consciousness

& the myth of time forever. The first time

we communed, I grew bigger from their vastness,

uncontrollable laughter at rainbows in the sky,

jewels & butterflies adorning their eyes,

the way they are sharp and soft

and young and old, and uncontainable

with secrets because they know healing

is meant to be communal

We have that psychic double-Cancer connection,

cry at the same time when we're apart,

text each other bok choy roses and call each other

the whole sun. A and I are going to build

a church one day and in the meantime

we swim in voracious ocean and dance on black sands

with the whole island watching us,

drumming djembes to the rhythm of our feet

D has whisked matcha for me every morning
we've spent together, packs patchouli oil and oracle
decks and a full gua sha set on trips
and I wonder if they know they are
every queer's wet dream and I wonder how a single human
contains such a colossal capacity for care

When D took us for a ride in the pacific northwest,
drove through mudslide mountains like strolling
through a park, I yelped at every pothole but knew
we were safe, Daddy D protecting
all their wives in the car, like how we speak
my favorite language of *none-at-all*
and with a touch, I feel their current and liquify

B and A and D and I want to live
on a commune with connecting cottages,
hang out with our titties out, eat fruit,
and love all day. We chose each other
and named ourselves aunties, family

without obligation, intimacy

without ownership, home

in the already ripeness of ourselves,

like wine-red strawberries bursting

with sweet because they have been skipped

on their vine

This whole world could crumble but together

we'd build an ark and bring the animals

with rainbow-shaded scales and unruly

manes and too-big wings and sail off

into the distant, untamable sunset

When It Floods

Each time your house floods
is a chance to build on higher ground

When those waters threaten to drown you again
not a drop comes near

Untouched, just watch
safe in your home
dry as kindling pine

Love Is a Revolution

I tried writing a "fuck you" poem
but I can't even—

For I was put on this earth to love
amidst the wrath of fear

To transform poison into portals,
openings that reveal the flavors of love:

Sometimes love is chocolate cake,
decadence you lick off the plate

Other times love makes you pucker
like *sinigang* my mother makes

A "fuck you" is a call to sharpen my sword,
refine wielding love in all its forms

When loving is a skill,
may our practice be a revolution.

Never underestimate the power
of removing your energy
from a situation.

Buffet of Boys

when I told the universe I was ready for love,

it presented me

           a smorgasbord

              of not-quite-right

unbeknownst to me,   each time I said "no thanks" to

        "hey wyd" texts

        obligatory pecks

        lukewarm liking

        sloppy slurring speech

        boyish behavior

        not-having-your-shit-together

        and any hint of thirst

I grew closer

               and closer   to

my one.

I Love the Trees in Brooklyn

I fall into autumn

like a long-awaited embrace

watch the sky split open

with the first crackles of rain

and it widens me, too

stretches time

like gray clouds swathed across horizon

The breeze caresses my shoulders

cool drizzle tickles my skin

I can't stop

watching the leaves

dance with the wind, how they're waltzing

like lovers who have kicked it forever

I love the "good mornings" here

the shades of melanin

the tree on my block

wearing a sign on his collar that states
"I AM YOUR NEW TREE"

I love the *abuelo* stooped over his walker
to savor lunch in the center of the sidewalk

The person who stopped in their tracks
to read a page of an open book tossed by trash
even the garbage is beautiful
in Brooklyn

One must learn to pause moments
in Brooklyn—
easier done when heat fades
and the soundtrack of the streets
melts into a language you know

Entering memories

is all I want to do

I want pieces of them

to lay roots in my brain,

their smile to make a home inside me

imprints on my thighs from their grip

insisting on staying

when I leave

memorize what

peace
gratitude
safety
love

feel like in your body

so you can return here
again

and again

and again

Dreamstate

slice into cake
knife becomes musical
in her hands
like the way she speaks
each word picked
from grassy field
chain-link of wildflowers
I want to adorn
my body with
focus floats me
into the clouds
the horizon is endless

How the Clouds Waited

how I arrived to an empty flat & dappled Nordic sun,

your warmth lingering in earthy incense and scrawled

invitation to an afternoon nap & cardamom bun

how you barreled in, opened up

the windows & stripped off the kitchen-worn clothes

and I wondered if you were flustered from

the biking or . . . ?

how you watched me, tasting

warm spice and butter, eyes glistening

as if it were your tongue

how we journeyed to the sight, and in seeing

my gaze more enchanted by its garden instead

you asked, *Do you want to go outside?*

how I lay in your lap on the peak of rolling green meadow

how you told tales of the year you didn't want the sun,

how I marveled

at your Everests, your pink & white

how you picked me

violet wildflowers as we rose

how we rose

how we heard a reindeer's final howls & paused

in death's presence . . .

how passage is peaceful with you

how we hugged that giant tree
said that tree must've seen some shit
said we wanted to become trees when we go

how we needed one day, just one full day?

how you suggested I pack for rain
but the canal breeze was crisp
the clouds plush and full,

how they waited there for us

the mind can convince itself into believing anything,

but your   Intuition
Body
Womb
Spirit
Energy

knows.

I Love You Beyond

She tells me she loves me, and I gasp. How can someone so good love me bare? She tells me, *You deserve it*, and something tired in me begins to protest. But my body believes more each minute. I stop thinking and my body knows. Her love is balm for knuckles that have only known fists. When love is about punishment it is not love at all. Her love is my roots feasting on a long drink of rain. I see the sanctity of someone with my colors and my divinity blooms, too. When love is about liberation it changes everything. A love in tenderness. In *I want to cook you a meal.* In hands washing my hair. In speaking without words. In *I promise to keep you safe.* She tells me she loves me, and I say, *I love you too.* I tell her I love her, and that the words are not enough.

Love is not:
>punishment
>power or control
>driven by fear
>earned
>questioning
>a mental gymnasium
>violence

Love is:
>a practice
>an infinite resource
>healing
>safe
>forgiving
>liberating
>generative
>world-building

Love can also look like:
>stepping away
>saying no
>care from afar
>not enabling
>loving yourself first

She Was (We Are) Christina Yuna Lee

a knife became the instrument
for her final breaths
taken from her own   kitchen drawer
one of us
taken

                the way you cut into
                   lemon pound cake
           was the first thing I noticed
             about you, your hands
        in easy dexterity   had me
                      taken

      a knife became the instrument

in his hands,   a clumsy

    staccato

          shrieking
more than forty   wails

    wicked
      cacophony

in your hands, my favorite symphony

orchestral masterpiece

precisely performed

movements of careful creation

a slicing

into flesh   into cake

her vessel
is lopped

into the tub

into meager headlines

into amygdala of

every

Asian woman

I read about her and of course
I think of you

our new year's eve disco
bubble bath   on loop

how I caressed
your flesh
into the tub

into lavender womb

a woman with my roots—
loving you
means loving me whole, too

your vessel
is sacred

exquisite home

bearer & birther   I

am in reverence

of what we carry

you rinse my hair clean,

baptism for seeing

how love needs

to liberate

a knife became the instrument

for loving us
with urgency

her flesh

is mine

they tear us open

and we grow gardens in our veins

What is life-threatening
is also life-giving.

Aspirations III

She is made of jade,

of the Earth—a synonym

for God.

My Beating Red

is four thousand seven hundred miles

across the Atlantic

in the pocket of her denim flares,

in the hurried hands of my father,

in the turn of *New York*

Times & Rachmaninoff pages,

in the wriggling body of my fuzzy guard,

ecstatic for my homecoming, even if my departure

had only been a few. My heart

is everywhere, at once, and so enormous now

it can cover continents.

I guess a consequence of vastness

is that I will always miss someone I love . . .

How to Forgive a Soul

I feel for someone

neck-deep in swamp,

how impossible it must be

to see that feigned power

is never worth the harm,

that I was never the enemy.

In a dormant place,

she knew I only had love to give,

and in sitting beside me for tea

in our once-green garden,

her myth of me

would crumble.

Things that are not your responsibility:

other people's urgency
other people's growth
other people's perceptions of you

Prayer

Meet yourself in the prairie,
engulfed in mountains
and Junegrass

at dusk,
listen to stillness

how it moves
how it shouts
how your tender, thumping heart
is louder
in nature's wild

at the mercy of our Earth,
may you find safety

here,
may you find everything.

Tree Glitter

Who needs TV

when you have the leaves?

The trees are showing off today—have you seen

the tangerine beauty

or the banana yellow with ruby tips,

you know—the ever-exploding firework

just outside your door?

The air must have been the same temperature

as my body—oh right, nature an embodiment of me

to the exact degree. So I paused to revel

in myself because the trees demanded it,

stood still while the wind swept gold

down my hair and ravished me.

Fallen foliage swirled down streets

as if the leaves were playing rain,

as if the leaves performed a surround-sound symphony

just for my arboreal, auditory pleasure.

This is the thing they try to recreate

with those newfangled headsets

in the whatever-verse,

yet here it all is,

here it has always been.

Dark Fantasies

Roo and I are walking when he lifts his leg to pee.
The homeowner sees that I am an Asian woman.
He pulls out a gun.

A demon from my past grows tired of sending
hate mail. He arrives at my doorstep to show me
how much pain he's in.

People I once communed with warp my truth
with gossip. The community I nurture turns cruel
and I am alone again.

The soul of the man who took his life in the Dick's
parking lot hitches a ride with me. It is eternally
searching for peace.

I believe I need to prove myself to be worthy
of love.

I study darkness like watching
a leggy centipede
crawl along my skin

I am terrified
but I am curious

The more I can hold fear,
the brighter I can feel light

In the shadow play,
a blueprint.

Meet You There?

We rise to news coverage of the latest, greatest love story.
Today, two 婆婆 fell in love late in life in a still-theirs
Chinatown. Each love story is us in another dimension. The
most frenzied part of our day is breakfast. We are making
wet scrambled eggs and *longanisa* and tomatoes soaked in
suka and garlic rice for a dozen of our soul friends. Everyone
is here. Everyone is safe. There is freshly baked sourdough
on the sun-drenched counter. Real butter. Blueberry mint
compote we simmered on the stove with too-ripe berries
found in the depths of our fridge. How easy it is for us to
make sweetness from the forgotten. MacBooks and phones
don't exist here, but the exalted, azure ocean does. Her tide
a rolling reminder that Mama Earth will always hold our
grief with an ancient strength. Friends are catnapping on
the plush, green grass. Reading poetry to each other like the
living room is a sold-out Carnegie Hall. Snuggling with
puppies strewn about the farmhouse because one of our
dogs just had babies. New life is everywhere. Laughter,
everywhere.

Love is the reason we're here.
It really is that simple.

M2 to Københavns Lufthavn

white white white white white white brown island girl with blue hair white white white white white

This, Too, Will Become a Memory

We sit on the hardwood floor, eating curried cauliflower,
our dining table a plastic box. You had just moved into an
oceanside place of your own in Amager and, effortlessly, it
became ours. Before meals, we meet nose-to-nose and
breathe, feeling the nourishment on the plates before us, the
nourishment pouring out of the other, all of it precious food
in a world dense with longing. It is the summer of learning
to be alongside each other. I am learning to be beside the
constant swirl of your energy, a sun-soaked boulder at the
soles of a rushing waterfall. You are learning to care for a
person who cries at the thought of the fatally injured
gosling in the pond by your work, its family congregating
across water to mourn its short life. We live with
magnificence, yet my favorite moments are simplicity with
you: sharing a whole bag of potato chips late-night on the
Metro, giggling at every little thing. You hurrying home to
me—out of breath, hair across your face, clutching a
handful of wildflowers you picked outside the flat. Slow
dancing in silence to the big, white moon. Things feel closer
here—bioluminescent, like the light of our love.

"I love America more than any other country in this world, and, exactly for this reason, I insist on the right to criticize her perpetually."

—James Baldwin

I Actually Miss America?

Last night I got served an ad for barf-colored

baked beans, and it made me miss America.

Americans need campaigns for baked beans

and toilet paper because we have a dizzying

array of choices over what we purchase at the

grocery store and what we wipe our asses with.

Americans need a *moment* in the ketchup aisle

to contemplate which condiment would be tastiest!

Do Americans know that ketchup dates back to

Imperial China, where it was made with fish guts

and soybeans? Shared along passage to Indonesia

and the Philippines, until the British took a liking to

its salty umami and a man in Philadelphia corrupted

its base with tomatoes? Americans create choice over

trivial things because we lack choice over freedom.

We never asked for the selection on the shelves—

we just need that one true thing. Americans create

choice over trivial things because we must prove

by producing—decadence and poverty, Americans

know no in between. We eat capitalism for breakfast,

colonialism with our fries, and the oppression is as

ordinary as a trip to the store. And despite all of this

chaos that distracts us from getting free, it's beyond me

how I truthfully can't wait to wipe my ass with

Charmin and chew over which chili sauce will make

my mouth water most, leap down my country's aisles

with a cart full of nonsense, like a madwoman,

like a miracle.

Linear time is a construct

Western society instated

to feel a semblance of control.

When Friendship Becomes Art

Three water signs flow all week and a portal to utopia is
opened. We are in the lush, green valley of Hudson, held
by August's warm embrace, and we are here to embody
the purest form of care: Go on, baby, throw a tantrum

      because you haven't eaten.   Go on, baby,

            cry into our arms

because you're scared.   Go on, baby, pose

      like you're Michelangelo's muse

         and we'll help you take artful nudes,

we'll even be

      the creative directors   and lighting

assistants,

      because there is nothing

         more worthy of worship

            than a queer Asian femme.

B said a true artist learns the rules to abandon them
and create something new. Otherwise, the person is
merely a practitioner. Together we create a world where
the parts we were taught to be ashamed of are revered.

Held up to the light until it catches the sun

and beams rainbows through every cut.

Go on, baby, give us your cranky, your kinky,

your silly, your hungry, your wild, your poor.

We lift our lamp beside the country door.

How to Escape the Matrix

1. Slow down. Linear time is a myth of capitalism. Don't attempt the persistent cadence of the colonizer's calendar (secret: it's impossible); flow with energy instead. Life happens in divine timing, and its unfolding cannot be rushed.

2. Remember that the rules are made up. What you were taught to believe about your role and responsibilities was established by the people with selfish agendas. In fact, these structures were deliberately designed so you lack the time & space to live into freedom, peace, and pleasure. What would your life look like if you chose your own adventure? Your own value system? Your own measure of success? Be patient with yourself as you untangle which beliefs were spoon-fed to you, and which are your soul's own.

3. There are things that don't matter (see: #2), and then there are things that really, really matter. Peace. Kindness. Reparations. Justice. Humanity. Sit with these. Move them up in your programming.

4. Crown your body as the ultimate authority, and use its features to transport you to the higher place (see: breath, movement, meditation). Your body has your ancestors' wisdom encoded in its DNA. Your body will never lie. Listen closely.

5. Commune with beings who are living in the higher place. Animals. Mother Earth. Soul friends who are on the path. Escape is more fun with comrades.

6. Trust. Every disappointment is a redirection. Each painful experience, a portal for ascension. The darkness, a necessary and natural balance to the light (secret: it's coming). Hold onto things a little less tightly. It will all make sense in due time.

7. Revel in your newfound space. The emptiness will feel uncomfortable at first because society has conditioned you to believe that busy = good, and silence = bad. They are afraid of what will happen when you meet your true self in the empty room, for this is the place where anything—*absolutely anything*—is possible. This is where you meet freedom. This is where you meet God. This is where you realize that freedom and God are innate within you. What will you create from here? Your answer is urgently needed.

Gentle reminder: Live life as you in the real world (and not as your avatar on the internet).

Morning Coffee Is a Portal

I sip the sweet on an almost-winter's day

gazing into a slate blue city oceanscape

Seldom sun sets the room aglow,

whispers to me of the summer

I had platinum hair, lay in a midnight hammock

with my love, engulfed in olive trees & jasmine

I think of the time I traipsed

through Turkey's turquoise coast

with her eyeing my morning coffee's movement

as she drove one-handed through city center chaos

and I realized I love someone wild

I sip and see the years I lived in my palace,

lived inside music and theories that lit me

like the devout Colorado sun streaming onto granite,

coaxing the words from my body each day

These days the stillness is uneasy

and delicious.

The divine is teaching me patience

so I am waiting more and doing less,

feasting on enough, and learning

that a lifetime can't be rushed.

This season my strands liken the drizzly Danish sky

I have been here before and yet it is new;

I breathe into the quiet blue.

It is in the stillness we find answers.
In simplicity, bliss.
In the present, everything.

Really Really Really Really Really Sad Poem

There is a thin trail of dirt on my new prairie dress,

a dusty moth smeared across the square white curtain,

house plants whose tips are crisped from the too-bright

light. I couldn't stay asleep because the house reeked

of fish and my stomach was shrieking, *I shouldn't have*

eaten that meat, and my fiancé's sadness imprinted

on my body like a pregnant ache.

We count down the days until she comes home

and the counting happens too slowly.

My phone marks the unanswered messages

and they are coming too quickly.

She takes inventory of the ocean between us,

there's only one, at least it's not two,

and for the first time, I curse the water.

I try to return to the place where there is

nothing worth counting barring

how many times we've made love in a day,

but instead I track the path of a fat black ant

wandering aimlessly across slate

in the not-quite September sun.

Recipe for Healing

Yesterday

> I learned that his dog, which was once our dog,
>
> had passed. D showed me a photo his mother
>
> posted on Facebook, zoomed in on the sweet lab's
>
> face, and I thanked D for what he left out of frame

It has been more than one thousand ninety-five days

since I started untangling

his grisly reality from mine and still,

I step toward the light

Today

> I searched "what is abuse in a relationship"
>
> erupted into lucid tears reading a fact sheet on
>
>> emotional & verbal abuse
>>
>> digital abuse
>>
>> stalking

These words have visited me

on my therapist's sofa

sitting beside soul friends

in seldom confessions of the depths of my endurance
and still

Belief hits different
when it comes from your own knowing

So each day I pray
Greet the sun with breath
Bare my soul onto the page

And slowly, the truths emerge:
There is no mistake that makes you unworthy of living
No amount of punishment that is just
No one who can claim your goodness is a lie

I am a miracle.

I am here

I am breathing

I am alive

I love the way I stumble

I love the way I learn

I love the way I live my life

I am in awe of my strength

I am in awe of my magic

I am in awe of my power

I am the whole sun,

embodied in human form

This is my gospel.

Love = Truth

Truth = Love

Asian American: An Etymology

I texted

my father

on Lunar New Year

to make sure

he was alive—

our culture's

most auspicious

celebration

became the deadliest

mass shooting

in the history

of Los Angeles.

The victims

were dancing,

like him—

in their golden years

when violence

waltzed

into our precious

town's ballroom.

I tried

to forget

superstition

that today's events

set the tone

for the year ahead

as I folded

my lucky dumplings,

built a small

mountain of clementines

for the daughters

who didn't hear back,

toasted over

the reluctant

altar

the meaning

of Asian American—

is to laugh and sob

mourn and rejoice,

to love

and be loved

all in a day's time.

Immigrant Gluttony

rice & soy sauce

weekly egg, if he was good—

my dad's childhood lunch

a classic of my parents'

immigrant tales, another is

> how my mom was the last

> of eleven to leave Manila—

> canonical to our legacy

> of sustenance. it explains why

>> she says you always send

>> people home with a Tupperware—

>> *it means they have to come back.*

>>> it explains why my dad

>>> would warn that what was left

>>> on my plate would predict

>>> my future husband's face—

I never wanted a husband

with an unclean complexion

so I'd wish for immaculacy

on my last grains of rice.

this is how dining

became my daily devotion.

beloved is the meal

we had on the side of the road

in Chiang Mai—sat down

next to two old ladies and said,

we'll have what they're having.

they had only a bucket of still

water to wash the dishes and still

the meal was just as momentous

as the three-star dinner in fairytale land

where we were served

art on a plate and ate

in a dreamstate, feasting

into the hours of the night.

if gluttony is a sin, then

i'm a proud sinner.

every meal a wicked

transgression, each bite

an homage to my ancestors' labor.

now my whole family eating

and we call it living

in this country,

we call it victory.

And Still, Bliss

early alarm / overslept / awoke in frenzy / taxi to restaurant/
loaded luggage / to airport / met 27 coworkers / to Helsinki/
layover / to Tokyo / puked twice at baggage claim / self-
transferred luggage hoard / to Osaka / awaited coworkers /
bus to Kyoto / unpacked luggage at restaurant / walked to
apartment / diarrhea for days / and despite

my stomach screaming
I giggle, thinking, *how do I say "the squirts" poetically?*

despite my broken
Japanese, joyous chitchat
with shopkeepers, *bijinesumen*, teenagers at Teramachi

despite my love working
from dawn till the moon reigns high

I find bliss

   walking the streets after-hours, arm around her waist
   stealing kisses in a culture where queerness is quiet

   I find bliss meandering Maruyama,
   marveling at its green as I sync my breath
   to the sound of the stream

cherry blossom mochi
with pickled flower on top—
I taste the way to balance
salt & sweet

rest my trunk

against that of a tree,

sink toes in cool water

and conjure sanctuary

awaiting the park's attraction: a weeping cherry tree.

"When I dare to be powerful,
to use my strength in the service of my vision,
then it becomes less important whether or not I am unafraid."

—Audre Lorde

Perennial

may my voice be a flower

never mind the spectators
who delight in my petals' unfurling
passersby who press noses
for a whiff of pollened bits

this magenta masterpiece
is just for me.

unbothered,
I make beauty from dirt
stretch toward sun as I turn
the soil beneath my feet

a flower has no secrets
no scheme but to bloom

as it's written into me
as my roots insist
even when the light is fleeting

Be My Guest

Please debate my syntax,

the tempo of my prose

Go line-by-line in analysis,

dissection of my syllables

Give me paper marked red,

your strongest critique

because I don't do mediocre

and workshops are rarely free

Please have a seat

while I recite my sonnet in court—

they're asking for my silence

but how else would a poet retort?

I'd bare my soul's message

into that tiny trial mic,

preach a word from the stand,

show the jury my light

Praise be to poetry

who says, *There's beauty here, too,*

for crowning my words worthy

of such hullabaloo

Art as pure reflection,

as body of water song

My voice is ocean's will,

though bodied all along.

You are not on this Earth to prove yourself to anyone
except your highest self.

I Am the Whole Sun

of course

everything flocks

to such a thing of beauty

planets and space dust,

meteors all the same—nothing

can resist the source

of genesis

her light biblical,

biological, brilliantly visible

even when the moon talks back,

even when the funk ferments

and the rot decays

and the rats scurry,

begging for a sliver

of her rays

The Best Human on Earth

Did you see how the internet

tried to cancel the Dalai Lama?

His boyish mischief untranslatable

to the Western world, so they occupied

his comment section with displaced anger,

called His Holiness something low, untouchable,

a synonym for scapegoat, untouchable,

a synonym for pedestal

And while I take no pleasure

in someone else's misfortune,

the cacophony brings me peace—

I could abstain from all indulgence,

vow never to sin, hell,

I could die for the cause and

the comment section

would still be a war zone

When we call someone God,

we forget there is God in each of us

When we call someone God,

we play the film of our lives

on someone else's screen

One spring evening I soaked my tired

shoulders in an onsen,

breathed in hinoki wood & wet gravel,

and found heaven amidst a storm

My body told me

the fear & fury

don't belong to me,

and since then I've kept on living,

smacking my lips as I'm fed

the fruit of life in the garden of joy

I've broken my back to grow

I bet you His Holiness

is doing just the same;

I bet you He's laughing, too.

Life is stunning precisely because we get
to experience the raw, messy, painful, powerful,
beautiful full spectrum of human experience.

Don't let *any of it* pass you by.

On Our Way

it is raining in July.
the white linen pants we left
on the balcony will get wet
again. everything pertaining
to nature is cyclical—
humans are not exempt.
Grace Lee Boggs asked,
"What time is it on the clock
of the world?" I lift my head
to the sky, and love
on the downpour.

Notes

I first read the phrase "the whole sun" in an article by Calin Amber and Margarita Ren titled "Constellations of Care: On Small Scale Solidarities," which was published in *The Margins* by the Asian American Writers' Workshop in February 2021. The article chronicles the voice notes of two friends during the resurgence of the Black Lives Matter movement and how they found community care through the "mundane" solidarity that exists in everyday friendship and outside of linear time. Ren calls Amber a "whole sun" as a term of endearment. Their friendship exudes this colossal depth; they fully embrace one another in all their complexity. My friend Angel and I started calling each other "whole suns" as we read this article together in a community we cultivated on Clubhouse, an audio-based social media app we frequented during quarantine. This expansive period of time when I was rapidly evolving as a person, as well as the limitless nature of self that is achieved through queer friendship, community care, and liberatory practices, are encapsulated in the phrase "the whole sun," and thus, it became the title of my book.

p. 9
"Home Has Never Been a Place" largely takes after Sally Wen Mao's poem, "Portable Cities,"

which I encountered during a workshop with Khadijah Queen.

p. 13

"What is, deeply, your to-do?" is a note I took while listening to an episode of *For The Wild* titled "On Humanity's Homecoming," which originally aired in September 2021. In it, Woman Stands Shining (Pat McCabe) encourages us to move away from modernity's obsession with intellectualism and toward a broader-spectrum way of knowing, a new world paradigm that places life—all life— at the center of our endeavors.

p. 19

"Women don't exist to jump from the hands of man to man" is a note I took after a session with Linda Hsieh, my therapist at the time. Linda was integral to my healing during one of the darkest chapters of my life, and I'm eternally grateful to them for their wisdom, guidance, and affirmation.

p. 23

"Freedom Dreaming" is inspired by the way in which Tourmaline speaks on the tradition in a July 2020 article for *Vogue* titled "Filmmaker and Activist Tourmaline on How to Freedom Dream." They write about the ways in which they freedom dream every day—"the everyday acts of liberatory glamour, care, and openness that keep us alive," which act as proof that, in many ways, we already live in the world we wish to create. The concept of freedom dreaming was originally put forth by Professor Robin Kelley and calls us to envision not what we are fighting against but what we are fighting for. It's a powerful practice that enables the grueling work of activism to be sustainable, pleasurable, and joyful.

p. 28
"Mourning After" was written the morning after eight people were killed by a gunman in Atlanta, Georgia, on March 16, 2021. Six of the victims of the Atlanta spa shootings were Asian women. Soon Chung Park, Hyun Jung Grant, Suncha Kim, Yong Ae Yue, Delaina Ashley Yaun Gonzalez, Paul Andre Michels, Xiaojie Tan, and Daoyou Feng—may you rest in peace.

p. 36
The concept presented in "Freedom" is inspired by Audre Lorde's essay "The Master's Tools Will Never Dismantle the Master's House," in which she urges women to refrain from operating within what heteropatriarchy deems acceptable, which will never bring about genuine change. Instead, women must embrace our differences as forces for meaningful change and forge intersectional community bonds— enabling us to create an entirely new world that exists outside of the systems that oppress us.

p. 37
During a 2007 interview with Bill Moyers, the activist Grace Lee Boggs said that "we need to embrace the idea that we are the leaders we've been looking for." The phrase was later adapted as a chapter title in her 2011 book *The Next American Revolution*, which is co-authored by Scott Kurashige.

p. 42
In "Year of the Tower (XVI)," the phrase "time is a mother" is the title of Ocean Vuong's 2022 poetry collection, published by Penguin Books.

p. 51
"Never underestimate the power of removing your energy from a situation" is a teaching I learned from Maryam Hasnaa, the founder of New Earth Mystery School. In a tweet posted on February 20, 2018, they wrote, similarly: "Sometimes the best way to help someone is to simply energetically walk away. Believe in the power of removing your energy. Trust that people will feel it and the message will be loud and clear."

p. 65
"She Was (We Are) Christina Yuna Lee" honors Christina Yuna Lee, whose life was taken on February 13, 2022, in her home in Chinatown, New York—and the collective grief felt by Asian women across the country.

p. 83
James Baldwin wrote this line in the
introduction to his 1955 essay collection,
Notes of a Native Son.

p. 87
In "When Friendship Becomes Art," the line
"We lift our lamp beside the country door" is
an ode to and play on the sonnet inscribed on
the Statue of Liberty—"The New Colossus"
by Emma Lazarus.

p. 89
I wrote "How to Escape the Matrix" while I was
reading *Notes on Shapeshifting* by Gabi Abrão.
The piece's list format and whimsical instructions
on how to live life were undoubtedly inspired by
Abrão's writing.

p. 102
"Asian American: An Etymology" is an homage
to the eleven lives that were lost during a
January 21, 2023 shooting at the Star Ballroom
Dance Studio in Monterey Park, California. A
city within what's lovingly known as "the 626,"
Monterey Park is dear to the Asian American
community and is largely comprised of Asian
seniors. Rest in peace My Nhan, Lilian Li,
Xiujuan Yu, Muoi Dai Ung, Hongying Jian,
Yu Lun Kao, Chia Ling Yau, Valentino Marcos
Alvero, Wen Tau Yu, Ming Wei Ma, and Diana
Man Ling Tom.

p. 110
This line appears in Audre Lorde's 1980 book,
The Cancer Journals.

p. 111
"Perennial" was written while I was listening to
the song "Perennials" by Emergence Collective,
a music initiative founded by Kate Douglas,
Matthew Dean Marsh, Raina Sokolov-Gonzalez,
and Sylver Wallace. The poem's title and resolve
to bloom are inspired by the song's lyrics.

p. 120
"What time is it on the clock of the world?" is a
question posed by James and Grace Lee Boggs in
their 1974 book *Revolution and Evolution in the
Twentieth Century*. The quote made its way to me
through the work of adrienne maree brown, who
was a student of Grace Lee Boggs. amb evoked
this question as a reminder to look at the bigger
picture while considering movement work—a
strategy for maintaining perspective, hope, and
optimism during difficult times.

Acknowledgments

To my editor, Melissa: thank you for believing in my writing and for shepherding this book through the publishing process with intention & care. When I began this journey, I wondered who my book's "mothers" would be. That we met when you were, quite literally, about to become a mother feels like no small coincidence. Thanks to you, the birth of this book is big and bright.

Thank you to Lighthouse Writers Workshop, which has been my literary home since the genre of poetry found me in the summer of 2019. Your belief in my potential and the support of your workshops & staff have helped me grow into a thoughtful, meticulous, and confident poet.

To my dad: thank you for loving me fiercely, cultivating my passion for writing & the arts, and instilling in me a relentless drive to live my best life. When the world feels unsafe, you remind me that I am supported, protected, and loved.

To my mom: thank you for every home-cooked meal, staying by me when I've hit rock bottom, and nurturing me into the warm, generous, and laughter-filled person I am today. It took me years of traveling the world to realize that home will always be wherever you are.

Thank you, Deets, for becoming another father to me. Not many people can say they've gained a father-daughter relationship later on in life. We are lucky. Thank you for your grounded presence, your sage advice, and for always being there with a fantastic bottle of wine.

To Justin and Stella: each time I've called with colossal news, you've shown me nothing but love & acceptance. Thank you for affirming who I am and celebrating with me as I've uncovered it.

To my family: this book reveals ancestral wisdom that has been in our bloodline for generations—I am merely the vessel for its delivery. This is for every ancestor who sacrificed so the next generation could live a better life; for the babaylans & indigenous keepers who were committed to healing despite persecution; and for our descendants who have yet to grace this Earth. I was divinely guided, protected, and grounded while writing these words because of the strength of our ancestry. Thank you.

I am grateful to the lineage of thought that has shaped my perspective, including (and certainly not limited to) adrienne maree brown's work on pleasure activism, Tricia Hersey's "Rest is Resistance" movement, the energetic teachings of Maryam Hasnaa, Ocean Vuong's wisdom on language as humanity's greatest technology, the

writing of Audre Lorde, and the work of bell
hooks, which altered my knowing of love.
I benefit from the labor of movement workers,
organizers, and artists who precede me; and
from the work of Black women—queer Black
women in particular—who have been crucial to
my journey of unlearning & activism.

To my queer family: Angel, Belinda, and Dove—
thank you for freeing me and helping me
discover my limitless nature. The way I feel in
our friendship is a blueprint for how I want to
feel all the time; how I wish everyone on Earth
got to feel; and how I know a world of radical
love, safety, and acceptance is possible.

To Niki, Jamie, Elyssa, Demi, Jaclyn, Sarah P.,
Sarah K., Michelle P., Michelle N., Natasha,
Ida, and Ashley—thank you for seeing me,
celebrating me, and giving me a soft space to
land when things aren't going my way. Without
you, I wouldn't be as radiant and as whole.

Thank you to my dog, Roo, for faithfully
guarding me through every season.

And to my love, Jocelyn: thank you for showing
me that true love exists, filling me up with food
& romance & adventure, and protecting my
tender heart from the harsh wiles of the world.
I'll never stop writing about our love.